WISLEY HANDBOOK 32

FERNS

REGINALD KAYE

LONDON
The Royal Horticultural Society
1978

Contents

Illustrations

Figs. 2, 3, 8, 9 by H. J. Bruty.

Figs. 5, 10, 23 by R. P. Scase.

Line drawings and all other photographs by R. Kaye. The line drawings were originally published in *Hardy Ferns* by R. Kaye, published by Faber and now distributed by the British Pteridological (Fern) Society.

FERNS

1. Ferns in the plant kingdom

Ferns belong to one of the larger divisions of the plant kingdom, the Pteridophyta, which also contains such plants as clubmosses, horsetails and quillworts. Although they possess well-developed vascular and supporting tissues comparable with those of the seed-plants, they differ in their reproductive arrangements.

The life-cycle of ferns demonstrates what is known as "the alternation of generations", because fern plants as we know them in the garden are neutral organisms which do not possess sexual organs, but which form minute reproductive bodies, the spores, which on germination do not directly produce a new fern plant. Instead, the spore develops into a small, independent, scale-like plant known as a prothallus, seldom exceeding an inch (2 cm) in diameter. On the underside of this prothallus male and female organs are formed, microscopic in size, and from the union of male and female cells a new fern plant develops. The two generations are designated the sporophyte generation, the neuter plant, and the gametophyte generation, the prothallus.

Some ferns are able to reproduce themselves by vegetative means, but the great majority are dependent on the alternation of generations for their propagation.

Each year a single fern plant may form many millions of spores which are distributed far and wide by the wind. Obviously, only a very tiny proportion of these spores succeeds naturally to produce new plants; otherwise the entire countryside would be invaded by ferns. Many spores land in hostile environments, but those which do fall in places suitable for growth may easily succumb to drought or be attacked by fungi, minute insects and the like, as they are very vulnerable in the first stages of germination.

Nevertheless, ferns are extremely successful, having evolved over some three hundred million years, until today there are something like 10,000 different species growing in the world, mostly in semi-tropical countries.

In our own British flora there are about fifty species to be found in various parts of the country, and there is a good number of exotic species from the temperate zones which will thrive in our climate.

The fern plant naturally varies in habit from species to species, but the majority form a more or less stout stock or "stem" which is covered by old frond bases below, terminating in the current year's fronds, spirally arranged

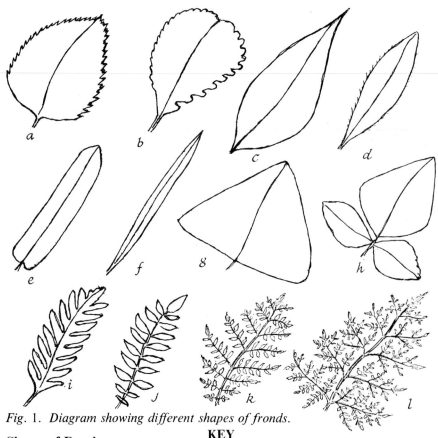

Fig. 1. *Diagram showing different shapes of fronds.*

Shapes of Fronds
KEY

a. Ovate, upper edge serrate, lower edge bi-serrate, apex acute.
b. Obovate, base cuneate, upper edge crenate, lower edge lobate, apex retuse.
c. Lanceolate, edge entire, apex acuminate.
d. Elliptic, edge ciliate, apex blunt.
e. Oblong, base cordate.
f. Linear, apex acute.
g. Deltoid—of general outline.
h. Deltoid, ternate, or trifoliate.
i. Pinnatifid, oblong.
j. Pinnate, lanceolate. Pinnae entire.
k. Bipinnate, ovate. Pinnae divided into pinnules.
l. Tripinnate, triangular. Pinnules divided into pinnulets.

4

around the growing point which is closely protected by the tightly curled new fronds formed to expand the following year. The new, uncurled fronds are usually densely clothed with scales. When the fronds expand they may be entire, as in the hartstongue fern but usually they are divided in varying degree in a feathery fashion. (For further details of 'Variation in British Ferns' see Section 10 of this booklet.) The frond is so termed as it is not simply an organ like the leaves of seed plants which transpire water vapour and build up food material by utilising solar energy. As well as these functions the fern frond also bears the spores in groups of characteristic shape according to the species, on the backs of the frond. The spores are formed in minute cases (sporangia) which themselves are grouped in clusters (sori) which are either naked or protected by a characteristic membrane (the indusium). The shape of these sori varies in different species and is used as one means of identification.

 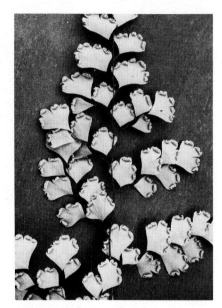

Fig. 2. Arrangement of sporangia on Asplenium frond.

Fig. 3. Arrangement of sporangia on Adiantum capillus-veneris.

Other ferns, instead of having a definite stock, grow by means of rhizomes, usually very slender, but in the case of bracken fairly stout, from which the fronds arise at fairly short intervals. These rhizomes usually grow under the soil surface, but those of *Polypodium* grow upon the surface.

The frond may be pinnate when the leaflets (or pinnae as they are termed) are divided right down to the midrib (or rachis), or bipinnate when the

5

pinnae themselves are so divided. If the pinnae divisions are themselves divided to their midribs, the frond is then described as tripinnate. In certain varieties of *Polystichum setiferum* the fronds are even quadripinnate.

The manner in which the young fronds uncurl, in the vast majority of species, is characteristic of ferns. They are popularly termed "croziers" or in American "fiddleheads". The technical description is circinnate vernation.

Fig. 4. Croziers of Polystichum setiferum Divisilobum unfurling in April.

2. Ferns in the wild

Over the many millions of years during which ferns have been evolving, the species have adapted themselves to many conditions, but in general, and especially in the case of the larger ferns, there is a marked preference for shady environments. Many ferns are plants of our British woodlands where they flourish, revelling in the cool humid atmosphere and the protection from high winds given by trees. Frequently woodland streams are edged by a dense growth of ferns, though few will thrive in boggy conditions. The royal fern, *Osmunda*, grows particularly well when its roots can reach the water, though the crowns grow well above the water level.

At the other end of the scale the tiny filmy ferns also are seldom found very far away from water and heavy shade—they need maximum humidity in order to flourish.

Fig. 5. A fine clump of Osmunda regalis growing at the water's edge at Wisley.

Many of the smaller ferns, especially the spleenworts (*Asplenium*), prefer growing amongst rocks in crevices where they get shade from the rocks, and a cool root run below them. When man came along and built stone walls with lime mortar the spleenworts adopted them with enthusiasm, and it is true to say that some spleenworts and the rustyback, *Ceterach officinarum*, are to be found growing in far greater numbers in walls than in other habitats, though almost always on the north or north-west sides out of direct sunshine. Hundreds of yards of our lakeland stone walls are crowned with dense growths of polypody. These are also found as epiphytes, growing on the mossy bark of woodland trees.

A few ferns have become adapted to growing in the open, especially in mountainous districts. *Cryptogramma crispa* is found in great abundance in the lakeland fells even in full sun, on stone walls, in screes and rock crevices, and even in the fell turf near streams where their roots can reach moisture.

Even such tender looking species as the oak and beech ferns, typically woodland ferns, will thrive high up the mountain sides, especially in deep gills but also under large rocks which keep off the sun. I have even found filmy fern growing in rock crevices on the Devonshire tors, stunted but able to survive by benefit of the moist sea breezes. Because of the prevailing winds off the Atlantic, the western regions of Britain have a much greater and more flourishing range of species than the drier eastern counties.

7

Two examples of ferns which prefer to grow in crevices.
Fig. 6. (above) Asplenium viride.
Fig. 7. (below) Ceterach officinarum crenatum.

Another favourite habitat of ferns is in hedge bottoms, especially those where the hedges crown banks of earth above sunken roads as seen so often in the south-west. Some species find congenial quarters amongst the debris around forsaken mine workings where some humus has formed amongst the rubble. One or two species confine themselves to sea cliffs especially where tufa has formed and there is a seepage of water down the rock crevices.

Then there is the effect of lime in the soil. While some species seem to prefer calcareous soils, especially the spleenworts (though not all), the shield ferns (*Polystichum*) and the rustyback, others seem indifferent, and there are those which will not grow except in acid soils. The last include the parsley fern, the mountain buckler fern (*Oreopteris limbosperma*), *Blechnum*, the oak and beech ferns. Notwithstanding the basic rock there are often acid patches left by glaciers on our limestones where *Blechnum* and other species may be found. Sometimes the soil above limestone has had the lime leached out of it and there are actually peat beds formed over limestone—in some places there are colonies of lime-hating plants thriving thereon.

3. Siting and preparation for planting

The first consideration is to find a really suitable position for planting. Where choices are limited in the small garden plot, a corner where direct sun does not fall, or does not get round until late in the day should be chosen. Such spots may be found on the northern side of the house, of a fence or garage. Alternatively, if there is a tree in the garden shading part of it during the heat of the day, a place where the flowering herbaceous plants do not thrive, then probably this will be as near ideal a site as may be found.

In larger gardens there are usually several areas with shady conditions, in bays between shrubs perhaps or on the shady side of trees, garden houses and the like.

The second consideration is protection from strong winds, particularly the cold draughts which often persist between adjacent houses, and the back draughts which often are found close to buildings.

Having chosen a suitable position the next job is to prepare the soil for planting. Many of the stronger ferns will tolerate poor conditions but it is much more satisfactory to give them a good start and have the satisfaction of seeing the plants grow into fine specimens which will give continued pleasure. The most important thing is to provide plenty of humus-forming material, whatever is available. The best is well decayed leafmould from oak or beech woodlands. If this is not obtainable, good bracken peat or any good peat which is not very fine may be used, well-rotted garden compost, or pulverised bark. Animal manure unless very well rotted (two or more years old) should not be used. The bed should be dug over to the depth of a spade, and as much humus-forming material, up to 50 % of the soil bulk in the case of very light soils, should be well-mixed into the whole depth of

9

the soil. A dressing of bonemeal, 4 oz. per sq. yd. (132 g. per m2), should be lightly forked in. Dry peat must be thoroughly soaked before mixing it in the soil, otherwise it may be weeks before it takes up enough moisture in the soil to be useful to the plants.

Very heavy and clay soils should be well worked, preferably two spits deep, and allowed to weather and settle before planting. The deeper cultivation encourages drainage and helps the surface soil to get into good condition.

The best times for planting are March–April and September–October, avoiding mid-winter when root growth is slowed down. Actually established ferns, especially container-grown ones, can be moved at almost any time except in times of drought. After planting, a good watering to settle them in should be all that is necessary until new growth starts. Then if the weather is warm and dry an occasional good soak will help the plants until they become thoroughly established. When established very little in the way of watering will be necessary, except in times of continued drought.

When planting, ferns with a rootstock should be planted deep enough to bring the growing point flush with or just above the soil level. Never cover the stock completely. With stoloniferous ferns remove an inch or two of soil from the area, wide enough to accommodate the plants, spread out the rhizomes and cover with an inch of soil and press gently level. Plants with surface rhizomes, such as polypodies, should not be covered with more than half an inch of soil, just sufficient to keep them firm until root action starts again.

The rock ferns, such as aspleniums, are not suitable for planting in such beds, and are best grown in rock crevices in the rock garden, facing away from the sun. I find they often thrive in scree beds in the shade of rocks. Scree beds are prepared by mixing the top spit of soil with at least half its bulk of stone chippings, as well as a liberal addition of peat or other humus. An ideal position for rock ferns, hartstongue, polypodies and the bladder ferns (*Cystopteris*) is a north facing dry wall, built with natural stone, with fern mixture used in the place of mortar, that is equal parts of loamy soil and peat, with a leavening of coarse grit if the loam is heavy.

Such a wall is preferably built against a bank as a retaining wall, leaning slightly back from the vertical, say two inches in a foot of height, on sound foundation stones, each course of stones placed on a thin layer of soil, levelled up behind the wall with similar soil made very firm by ramming. After 9 inches height is achieved the ferns may be planted as the wall is built, wedged between adjacent stones with soil, the plants about a foot apart.

A double wall could be built instead of a retaining wall, reserving the shady side for ferns, the sunny side for rock plants. The bottom stones in a double wall should be about three feet apart, from face to face, tapering inwards as building progresses so that a wall three feet high would be two feet across at the top. Occasional "through" stones, that is stones long enough to span from face to face, should be included to hold the faces apart. Very firm filling is essential, and only a thin layer of soil applied between courses so that the stones can "bite" together.

As with the ferns it is advantageous to plant the rock plants as the work proceeds. Holes left for later planting invariably allow rain to wash out the soil, weakening the structure. When walling always use the larger sides of the stones as faces, wedging them firmly in position with stone fragments, tapped tight with a hammer. The tops of the wall may well be planted with polypodies which love to crawl amongst the stones and bind them firmly. Occasional top stones wide enough to reach both faces, will also help to keep the wall stable. I built such walls about fifteen years ago, still a joy to examine, with lots of self-sown spleenworts—and ramondas—cropping up. Unfortunately I built them too near some trees which provide shade but their roots have invaded the soil behind the wall and tend to draw away too much moisture in times of drought.

4. Growing ferns in pots

In the long term ferns generally grow much better in the open garden than in pots, but there is no reason why they should not be grown in containers of some kind if they can be kept in a fairly shady place, and watched carefully to make sure that they never get dried out, while at the same time avoiding overwatering which tends to encourage sour soil. The cultivation of ferns in pots is best confined to the smaller-growing species, and for bringing on young plants for subsequent planting out. To keep the larger ferns growing well in pots involves potting on into larger sizes as they grow until a stage is reached where the labour of moving the pots becomes too much work. Once such pots get dry, often it is not possible to thoroughly moisten the root ball by overhead watering and it may be necessary to stand the pots in a tank of water to be sure of complete soaking. My favourite compost for potting ferns is made up by thoroughly mixing one part by volume of good loam, two parts of flaky leafmould, and one part coarse sand. To each bushel of compost is added a six-inch potful of granulated charcoal, one three-inch potful of hydrated lime, and a two-inch potful of John Innes base fertiliser. The lime is omitted when species that like an acid soil are being potted. But where these materials are hard to find, the various peat-based, soilless composts are very good for pricking off and potting on young plants, if the watering is carefully watched. Once these composts have dried out they need to be thoroughly soaked before the root ball takes up water again.

Ferns in my experience do best in earthenware containers, which are now being made by some of the smaller potteries, but the more readily available plastic pots are satisfactory if good drainage is provided, and care is taken with the watering. Large specimen plants can be grown in tubs or half-casks, these are suitable for placing in a shady patio. Such places as cold fruit

11

houses, vineries, greenhouses which have become shady through growth of neighbouring trees, and cold frames in the shade are very suitable for housing a collection of ferns which need slight protection, but hardy ferns should not be grown in the greenhouse for long periods, as they tend to be more susceptible to pests and diseases, and also grow out of character.

5. Ferns in the house

The filmy ferns, our two British ones, *Hymenophyllum* and *Trichomanes*, and several exotic filmy ferns, can be grown to perfection with very little trouble in a suitable environment, and the invention of the Wardian case meets their requirements very well. Essentially a Wardian case consists of a more or less airtight glazed cover to a shallow container of moist soil, in which plants can grow for months without any attention, as there is no water loss; all the moisture which evaporates during the warmth of the day condenses at night and runs back into the soil. In this way the enclosed air is maintained at maximum humidity, so important in the cultivation of filmy ferns. The same effect is obtained by covering a pan of ferns with a bell jar, if this can be obtained, but a more ornamental arrangement can be made in the Wardian case. This can be made to any convenient size, but if it is to be kept in a dwelling house it should not be too big to move easily, and its supports should be strong enough to carry the weight. The compost for pots mentioned on page 11 plus an extra part of sharp gritty sand to keep it more open will be satisfactory.

The bottle garden has the same principle of a closed self-supporting community; clear-glass carboys, large battery jars, and large sweet jars will all serve. In the case of carboys it is essential to use sterilised compost, otherwise a luxuriant germination of weed seedlings will create problems of extraction through the narrow neck. The carboy should be thoroughly cleaned before introducing the soil, which should be on the dry side so that it will run down into the jar bottom without sticking to the sides, to a depth of three inches or so. Then with a funnel with rubber tube attached run in a little water and leave it to permeate the whole soil, which should be just moist. The plants must be small enough to work through the carboy neck, and they can be manipulated and planted by means of a notched narrow lath and a cane. Four or five plants will be ample.

Be careful not to choose plants which might grow too large for removal later. Filmy ferns, spleenworts, and the dwarf forms of hartstongue are suitable.

6. Maintenance

Hardy ferns need very little in the way of maintenance, as they require no staking, and seldom need watering when once established, except in times of drought. The plants in nature receive a natural mulch from the autumn leaf-fall from the shade trees and build up humus from the remains of their own dead fronds, but in the garden it is advisable to provide a good mulch once or twice a year. The most important one is applied in the spring before the ground has dried out, after the plants have been tidied by removing the dead fronds from the previous season. In the case of deciduous species the dead fronds may be pulled away safely, but the old withered fronds of wintergreen and evergreen species should be cut away at ground level, as they generally are too tough to pull off without damaging the crown. Then apply bonemeal at 4 oz. per sq. yd. (132g. per m²). As soon as this has been done apply the mulch to a depth of about two inches. The mulch may be rotted leafmould, spent hops which have been stacked for three or four months, old compost mixed with granulated peat, or bracken peat.

Some ferns, especially the lady fern, *Athyrium*, after a few seasons in the garden tend to grow with the crowns above the ground level, as a result of normal growth and removal of some soil by weeding. When this happens either replant the ferns back to the ground level or increase the mulch to cover exposed stocks. The new roots are issued immediately below the fronds and will suffer in dry weather unless covered.

In any case every three or four years those ferns which make multiple crowns should be lifted and divided, for the plants look much better grown as single crowns. The extra crowns can be planted elsewhere in the garden as reserves. When several crowns are left together the fronds get tangled together and lose some of their grace. As mentioned above, watering is necessary only in very dry weather, and then an occasional heavy soak will be beneficial. A good mulch in spring will keep the ground below moist enough in most years.

The second mulch is applied in autumn, about the end of September. This is also the best time to replant any plants which need moving or rearranging.

The only other point to observe is to prevent weeds getting a hold, by early removal. As ferns make their new roots near the surface it is important to refrain from hoeing or forking very near the crowns; any forking to remove perennial weeds should be done with great care, just sufficient to allow the weed roots to be drawn out intact. If perennial weeds get into the crowns of ferns it may be best to lift the plant completely, carefully work out the weed and replant to the correct level.

7. Propagation

Vegetative Propagation

The simplest method of increasing a stock of ferns is by simple division of the crowns, or by division of the rhizomes, making sure that the rhizomes have growing points. In the case of some special varieties which will not come true from spores, or the plumose varieties which often are sterile, this may be the only way to increase stock. When a plant has developed several crowns, these should be separated by carefully lifting the clump, shaking off as much soil as possible, then inserting two border forks, back to back, between the crowns taking care not to get the tines through a crown, then by drawing the fork handles together gently prising the crowns apart. Usually the crowns will all be joined to a common stock at their bases. When all the crowns are separate, trim off any dead stock, and remove most of the lower old frond bases so as to allow intimate contact with the soil for the remaining rootlets, and replant. The rhizomatous species usually shake out very well, leaving a network of rhizomes. These will have small clusters of tightly rolled fronds at their extremities. Bits of rhizome without growing points are unlikely to form them, and may be discarded; those with growing points should be replanted by removing an inch or so of soil, spreading out the rhizomes with room to develop, and replacing the soil. Settle the soil around the plants by a good watering, after which the ferns will look after themselves.

Occasionally bulbils appear on the frond bases of species of *Dryopteris* and *Polystichum* and these grow into small plants which can be detached and grown on. If left they eventually grow into normal sized plants contributing to a mass of crowded crowns. But in the case of the 'Acutilobum' and 'Divisilobum' varieties of the soft shield fern, *Polystichum setiferum*, the whole midrib (rachis) can develop bulbils along its entire length, a score or more little brown knobs to each frond, and these can be induced to grow into small plants if the frond is detached and laid on a compost of sandy peat in a shady cold frame or cloche. It is as well to pin the frond into close contact with the sand by means of bent wires or old fashioned hairpins. Or the frond can remain attached to the plant and sandy peat placed under it, the frond pinned down as before. Eventually when the tiny ferns are well rooted and sending up fronds, the plantlets can be gently detached and grown on in a cold frame until large enough to plant out. One good sized parent plant can yield up to a hundred young plants in this way. Only robust, freely growing specimens form bulbils, so it is advisable to encourage strong growth by mulching with leafmould containing a little bonemeal three or four times a year.

The hartstongue, *Asplenium scolopendrium*, is a special case, for when the fronds die down, their bases remain plump and green for years. If a plant is lifted, washed free of soil, and these old frond bases are removed they can be induced to form bulbils by sowing the bases on sterilised peat-sand mixture, and keeping them in a closed environment in a shady greenhouse. I usually use plastic seed-trays covered with a sheet of glass cut to fit, and the whole enclosed in a clear plastic bag. These will keep moist for months without disturbance. Eventually each frond-base forms little white pimples which grow into tiny plantlets. When these are large enough they are detached, pricked off into ordinary fern compost, and grown on until they are large enough to plant out. Of course, there is no need to go to this trouble with the type species, or with those varieties which breed true from spores; sowing will provide more plants in a shorter time. But the plumose

14

varieties, such as *Asplenium scolopendrium* 'Crispum' in its various forms, are sterile, forming no spores (with one or two exceptions) and while the original crowns can be divided every two or three years, the frond bases can form from one to ten plantlets each, or one to two hundred per tray.

Of course, it may take three years growing on to get saleable plants in this way, after the first pricking off.

Any extra good varieties even though fertile, cannot be relied upon to come exactly similar from sowings, though even better forms may crop up. To raise stock exactly like the parent, the bulbil method should be employed.

Spore sowing

When large numbers of plants are required, especially in the case of original species, spore sowing provides the best means for working up large stocks. Probably the best time for sowing is in early spring, in March, then the young plants will have eight months in which to develop before cold weather stops growth, though if a greenhouse which excludes frost is available the plants can be kept growing through the winter. But first the spores must be harvested.

As mentioned on page 5 the spores are contained in minute cases, the sporangia, which themselves are grouped in tiny clusters on the backs of the fronds, the sori. These should be examined with a lens from time to time to ascertain their stage of development. As soon as they seem to be ripe, a portion of a frond bearing sori is detached and covered until the spores are shed. I use sheets of white sulphite paper, placing the frond flat, and folding the paper three or four times, writing the name on the paper, then storing in an airy place until the spores shed. This usually takes place within a week of gathering. On examination the paper will be found to be covered with dust-like spores—the single spore is quite invisible to the naked eye— and these are tapped into a heap on a small square of clean paper, folded up and packeted with the name and date. They are then stored in a cool dry place until there is a batch of varieties ready for sowing. As a guide to catching the spores before they are shed, *Osmunda*, royal fern, starts the season at the end of May to mid-June. Incidentally, this is a special case as *Osmunda* spores remain viable for less than a week at ordinary temperatures. Either sow them straight off the plant, or store the spores in a refrigerator until a convenient time. I have kept them a year in the freezer and got good germination. Nearly all other spores can be kept safely for six months or more in a cool dry store.

Then in late June and July, the shield ferns, *Polystichum*, ripen. *Cystopteris* are also ripe about this time. In August *Dryopteris* begins to ripen, followed by *Asplenium* and *Athyrium* into September. If sown when fresh, prothalli

Fig. 8. Sporangia in the correct condition for gathering spores with the cells still shut. (See over page)

may be formed before the winter, but are unlikely to produce young ferns before the following year unless kept in a frost-free house.

To be successful in raising ferns from spores it is essential to make a clean start by using sterilised containers and compost. In nature probably less than one spore in a thousand succeeds in producing a fern plant. The method I use is to prepare sufficient seed-pans by thoroughly scrubbing and cleaning them, place a piece of perforated zinc over the drainage hole, this covered with a piece of broken pot, concave side down, then either an inch of broken pot, or stone chips. I sieve some fern compost through a $\frac{1}{4}$ in. sieve, cover the drainage with the roughage, then top up to about two inches with the fine sieved soil, press down level and firm, cover with a piece of paper to prevent disturbance, then pour boiling water through the compost, up to the brim of the pan, until the pan is too hot to hold. Allow to cool, covering the pan before cold with a circle of glass. As soon as cold, take off the glass and sow the spores. A tiny heap on the point of a knife blade is ample. Tap the knife a few inches above the pan (in a place where there are no draughts), label with a new label, cover with glass, and place on a layer of chippings on a shady bench in a cold greenhouse. A 5-in. pan will accommodate over 200 prothalli with ease. The glass covers are cut from pieces of broken glass by inverting the pan on a piece of glass on a level surface, and running around the edge with a glass-cutter. A few taps and the unwanted glass breaks away, leaving the glass circle ready for use. A run round the edge with a file or hone will remove any sharp edges. Pots of 3 and $3\frac{1}{2}$-inch sizes are large enough for most purposes unless large numbers are required.

Such a pan will remain damp enough in a cool shady house for several weeks without further attention. The spores germinate, as a rule, in six weeks or so and appear as a thin green film, later forming the prothalli. The first young fern fronds may appear a month or so after the prothalli have matured. The glass cover is never removed until the new fronds appear, any watering is done by standing in water in which a few crystals of permanganate have been dissolved. This method has been used by me for many years but there is no reason why other containers might not be used, the plastic cartons used for ice-cream are quite good, the plastic covers can be used instead of glass. Having no drainage it is advisable to include a little granulated charcoal in the compost, which must be sterile before putting in the container. The boiling water method could not be used with such containers. The compost should be just damp enough to break up without becoming muddy when disturbed.

If the prothalli come up too thickly to develop properly they will have to be pricked off into similarly sterilised pans, in little tiny bunches, half an inch or so apart, and kept in closed conditions until they develop. Having no roots it is rather a tricky business getting them to stand up. Water by soaking from below. When the tiny fern plants are an inch or so high they

17

should be pricked off to an inch (2.5 cm) apart and kept in a closed atmosphere until they grow freely, then they may be pricked out to two inches (5 cm) apart, and grown until they are large enough to pot off into thumb-pots. When large enough they may be planted out or potted on as wished. A record should be kept of all sowings tabulated as follows:

Date sown	Date first signs	Date prothalli formed	Date fronds appeared	Date pricked off	Date potted

with a further column perhaps for results and comments.

Fig. 9. *Pricking out sporophytes of a pteris.*

Hybridisation of ferns

Ferns do hybridise in nature and several natural hybrids have been recorded in Britain. Generally the horticulturist is more interested in obtaining hybrids from ferns which have already sported in some way, rather than crossing species. Successful crossing depends on the two participants having the same chromosome number, and this is more likely in the case of two varieties of the same species, than with two separate species. The chromosome numbers of species may be obtained from most modern botanical books, but the varieties which have horticultural interest are not given serious attention by botanists.

One method is to sow spores of two or more varieties of the same species, mixed together and hope for the best. The record book is useful here as varieties which germinate and produce prothalli at the same time have a better chance of hybridising.

18

A more scientific method is to grow the prothalli separately, and when these are nearly mature, the wider notched end of all the prothalli from both pans are cut out with a fine razor blade and transferred to their opposite numbers. The notched wider end of the prothallus contains the female archegonia, the narrower end the male organs, the antheridia. In this way there is a better chance of hybridisation taking place though it is impossible to guarantee success.

Another method is to flood one pan of prothalli with water at about 70°F. and after half an hour decant the water amongst the prothalli of the second partner. The water is likely to be full of motile male cells which may fertilise the archegonia of the second partner before its own antheridia discharge their own motile male cells, but there is a great element of luck in all these methods whether any hybrids are secured. One can only grow on the young plants when they appear, and judge from their appearance whether hybridisation has been successful.

The difficulty is that all the processes involved are quite microscopic, and cannot be controlled by manual manipulation, which is so comparatively easy in the case of flowering plants.

8. Pests and diseases

Ferns are seldom attacked by the general run of garden pests in the open, the chief enemies being slugs, snails, and woodlice which may attack the young tender fronds when first they begin to unfurl in spring. A scattering of slug bait around the plants when growth is beginning will ensure little damage from these creatures. Woodlice are sometimes pests amongst tiny seedlings which they may eat off. Carbaryl may be dusted around the seed-pans with good results; care should be taken not to get the substance on the ferns themselves, as it may cause some damage. Aphids sometimes infest the young growths of *Adiantum*, and dusting with derris is effective, but many sprays are injurious to young fern fronds, in fact spraying of any kind is detrimental to ferns, especially aspleniums, it can cause blackening of the fronds. Vine weevil grubs sometimes cause trouble; watering the ground with a BHC preparation will clear these, if taken in time. I have never come across the maggot which is said to attack the stems of lady fern and polypody, boring down the stems and causing discoloration and collapse of the frond above. It is said that removal and burning the fronds, picking them below the affected place, is successful in controlling attacks.

Birds can be a pest in spring, scratching up the mulches in search of food and possibly uprooting small recently planted ferns. A careful watch and replanting at once should save the plants. Moles can be a real nuisance, burrowing under fern beds, heaving up plants, and leaving airspaces below the plants preventing good root action. These are best dealt with by a pest eradicator from the local council. Sheep should at all costs be excluded from woodlands planted with ferns, for they will level every fern to the ground in a short time. This was brought home to me recently when examining a woodland famous for ferns in lakeland. After many representations the owners finally fenced off the greater part of the wood. As a result there was a marvellous development of ferns of all kinds in the protected area; in the unprotected part it was just bare ground and tree trunks, not a fern in sight.

9. A selection of Hardy Ferns

There are large numbers of hardy ferns from all the temperate parts of the world which might be grown in gardens, including the fifty or so species which are native to Britain.

Adiantum. The maidenhair ferns.

Many exotic maidenhairs are much hardier than our native *A. capillus-veneris*, and are among the most attractive species for the garden.

A. hispidulum. New Zealand, Australia, Asia. Rosy maidenhair. Similar to *A. pedatum* in that the fronds are pedate, with the pinnae arranged like the fingers of an outspread hand. Young fronds bright reddish pink, becoming dark green and rather leathery when mature. Evergreen in a frost-proof house, it will survive out-of-doors in sheltered districts, and is reported as an escape, established in Devon. 6–12 in. (15–30 cm).

A. pedatum. North America. This handsome species is absolutely hardy and appears self-sown in my garden in North Lancashire. The rhizome is creeping, sending up fronds at very short intervals, the fan-like blades disposed at an angle to the slender polished purplish black stems. *A.p. aleuticum* is a dwarf species from the Aleutian Isles, and North America, making mounds of rather glaucous greenery up to 6 in. (15 cm) high. A splendid rock garden species. 'Klondyke' is perhaps the tallest, up to 2 ft. (60 cm) high or more in a good environment. A worthwhile addition to the fern garden.

A. venustum. Kashmir and Canada. Not unlike our native species, with rather smaller pinnae, this species runs about making mats of beautiful slightly glaucous foliage. It gives a bonus in winter when the dead fronds persist, a brilliant coppery brown. The young fronds are pink. 4–5 in. (10–12.5 cm). Surface rooting, resents the rhizome buried more than $\frac{1}{2}$ inch (12 mm) below the surface. Likes humus-rich soil.

Asplenium

The British species are all rock ferns and colonisers of old mortared walls. They make good rock garden plants, more or less evergreen. All the spleen-worts need a very gritty compost, well drained.

A. adiantum-nigrum, black spleenwort, narrowly triangular, rather leathery fronds, 6 to 10 inches (15 to 25 cm) long.

A. ceterach see *Ceterach officinarum.*

Fig. 10. Adiantum venustum in the Alpine House at Wisley.

A. ruta-muraria, the wall-rue spleenwort, is found in most parts of Britain, nearly always in old walls. Dislikes pot culture, but does well in shady limestone scree.

A. scolopendrium, until recently named *Phyllitis scolopendrium*. This is the hartstongue, a very characteristic fern of the limestone "clints" of the north, but common all over Britain on basic soils. The leathery, oblong, bright green fronds are entire and wintergreen, and may be anything from 9 in. to 2 ft. (22.5 to 60 cm) long according to conditions. This fern has yielded many good garden varieties and is a splendid plant for the larger rock garden, at the base of dry walls, or in the shady border. There are many varieties, with variation in leaf form.

The green spleenwort, *A. viride*, is a true mountain fern, always on basic rocks, and makes a nice specimen in limestone scree.

A. trichomanes, the maidenhair spleenwort, is common throughout Britain, away from industrialised areas. It is a very good rock fern in the

Fig. 11. *Asplenium scolopendrium 'Nobile'.*

garden and grows well as a pot plant, in fern compost to which lime-mortar rubble has been added. There is a crested form, which comes true from spores.

Athyrium

A. filix-femina. The lady fern is one of our commonest ferns, which contributes in no small way to the beauty of our woodlands, the large lanceolate fronds are bipinnate, and may exceed 3 feet (90 cm) in length. Over 700 varieties have been recorded, but most of them have disappeared; the following are really good ones.

A. f-f. 'Frizelliae'. The tatting fern, found in Ireland about 100 years ago. The pinnae are reduced to little green balls, giving the frond the appearance of a string of beads. A charming variety, seldom exceeding 12 inches (30 cm). It comes quite true from spores.

A. f-f. 'Plumosum'. Really a section, many forms have been found and raised. The fronds are at least tripinnate, especially feathery and of a lucent almost golden-green. Often sterile but when spores are formed they reproduce the form faithfully, with an occasional crested variant.

22

Fig. 12. A variety of Athyrium filix-femina plumosum, called Penny's variety.

A. f-f. 'Victoriae'. Probably the most extraordinary wild find ever made, found in Scotland about 100 years ago. The original clone is rare now, sporelings retain the habit but seldom reach the magnificence of the original which may have fronds up to 3 ft. (90 cm) in length, narrowly lanceolate, perfectly cruciate and crested.

A. niponicum. Japan. A most attractive species, most often seen in its variegated variety 'Metallicum', originally known as *A. goeringianum* 'Pictum', the Japanese painted fern. The frond, bipinnate, can be from 12–24 in. (30–60 cm) long, midrib wine-red, the pinnae soft grey with wine-red midribs, merging to grey-green at the margins. The black spores germinate, producing about a third 'Metallicum' and two-thirds normal *A. niponicum.* Seems quite hardy in Lancashire, sending up new fronds till late autumn.

Blechnum

B. penna-marina is from New Zealand. A tiny creeping species which makes mats of dark green, roughly textured pinnate fronds 3–4 inches (7.5–10 cm) long. Hardy all over Britain.

23

B. spicant. The only British species, the hard fern, is a lime-hater, found only on acid soils, but common. Requires a moist soil. More or less evergreen. The narrow fronds are set with pinnae like the teeth of a comb.

B. tabulare (*Lomaria magellanica*). South America. This very handsome species was introduced over 200 years ago. The creeping rhizome forms crowns at intervals sending up immense fronds up to 4 ft. (120 cm) high. Deep glossy green, pinnate, the young fronds often copper tinted, keeping green well into the winter. The rhizomes creep about making an underground network excellent for stabilising the banks of streams. Extensive plantings may be seen in Savill Gardens at Windsor.

Ceterach
C. officinarum. Rusty-back. A dwarf limestone fern eminently suitable for the rock garden. Dwarf, evergreen deeply-lobed linear-lanceolate fronds, 3–6 in. (7.5–15 cm) long, reverse side covered with silvery scales becoming rusty-brown. For every plant found on natural rock, a hundred will be found on old mortared walls. Now often regarded as an *Asplenium*.

Cryptogramma
C. crispa. Parsley fern. A true mountain fern on acid soils, a lime-hater. Very common in lakeland, perhaps the dominant fern in some areas, in shade and full sun. Quite deciduous, the cheerful bright-green deeply divided, 4–6 inch (9–15 cm) fronds show up very well in spring. Can be grown in pots in acid compost lightened with granite chips, or in peat walls.

Cystopteris
The bladder fern. So called on account of the domed indusium covering the sorus like an inflated hood.

C. bulbifera. The narrowly triangular fronds may be from 6 in. to 3 ft. (15–90 cm) long according to environment. Deciduous. Bears bulbils on the frond backs, affording a ready means of increase. From North America.

C. fragilis. A very brittle-stemmed fern, the 6 in. (15 cm) fronds snap off very easily. Common in British mountains, and sows itself freely in rocky situations. Quite deciduous.

C. regia. Beautifully dissected emerald fronds, 4–6 in. (10–15 cm); like the other species needs shade to keep its colour. Deciduous.

24

Dennstaedtia

D. punctilobula is from North America. Can be invasive in good conditions, the creeping underground blackish rhizomes run about throwing up the very beautiful tripinnate fronds to about 18 in. (45 cm). The fronds have numerous glandular hairs exuding a pleasant scent. Fine for stabilising soil.

Fig. 13. *Cryptogramma crispa* (*the parsley fern*).

Dryopteris

The buckler ferns. Getting the name from the kidney or buckler-shaped indusium, these mostly are large easily grown ferns on any soil, all deciduous.

D. carthusiana. Spiny buckler fern, narrow buckler fern. Widespread but local, usually on acid formations. A graceful fern, the stem usually longer

25

than the blade, which is narrowly triangular to lance-shaped, the pinnae sharply toothed. The creeping rhizome rather slender, crowns covered with very pale brown scales. Usually in wet woodlands, heaths and marshes.

Fig. 14. *A variety of the male fern; Dryopteris filix-mas Decomposita.*

D. austriaca. Broad buckler fern. Usually on acid formations, makes large plants with fronds up to 4 ft. (120 cm) long, broadly triangular, tripinnate, especially in damp woodlands. Very dark brown scales cover the unfurled fronds. One or two varieties still exist.

D. filix-mas. Male fern. Probably the commonest native, sowing itself freely in gardens, found all over Britain. Too robust for the small garden, but admirable for naturalising in woodland. Many varieties, mostly coming true from spores. Among them are 'Cristata' and 'Linearis', a tall variety up to 3 feet (90 cm) with very slender reduced pinnae, giving an airy effect. Well worth a place in any garden.

26

D. pseudomas. Golden-scaled male fern. Until recently named *D. borreri,* now replaced by its older specific name. Distinguished from *D. filix-mas* by the glossy, rather leathery, sub-evergreen fronds, stems covered with conspicuous shaggy orange-brown scales. A fine sight in lakeland in spring when the bright golden-green croziers are unfolding. Has several good varieties, including 'Cristata The King' which has splendid symmetrically crested arching fronds up to 3 ft. (90 cm), and 'Ramosissima Wright' whose fronds branch repeatedly and terminate in large handsome crests. A first class variety, making a large bush.

There are several Japanese species which are reasonably hardy. *D. ery-throsora* is the best. The young fronds come up in spring a vivid coppery-pink, turning yellowish green as the frond matures, 18–24 in. (45–60 cm). The sori are covered by bright red indusia when ripe. It requires a deep humus-rich soil, in dappled shade. The other Japanese species I grow, *D. sieboldii,* looks more like a giant *Pteris* than a *Dryopteris,* but the sori are characteristically dryopteris-like. It has an immense terminal pinna, 8–12 in. (20–30 cm) long, up to 2 in. (5 cm) wide, glaucous green, supported by two or three pairs of smaller pinnae below. Good deep soil and protection from strong winds encourage strong growth, fronds 18 in. (45 cm).

Gymnocarpium

G. dryopteris. Oak fern. Perhaps the loveliest of British ferns, the soft golden-green deltoid blade is tripinnate, set on long stems, arising at short intervals from the slender creeping rhizomes which form a network just under the ground surface. Usually in acid woodlands. 9–12 in. (22.5–30 cm). Deciduous.

G. robertianum. The limestone polypody is a leathery, harder-textured version of the oak fern. Runs about amongst stones very freely.

Hymenophyllum

Filmy Fern. These delicate moss-like ferns are found in damp woods, on tree trunks and rocks frequently damped by spray from waterfalls, in areas of high humidity. Can only be grown in Wardian cases, under belljars or similar structures.

H. tunbrigense. Evergreen, pinnate fronds, 2 in. (5 cm), with irregular segments.

H. wilsonii. Much commoner. Narrower segments, the pinnae branching one side more than the other. The translucent fronds, but one cell thick, suffer severely if allowed to get dry.

Fig. 15. *Dryopteris erythrosora, one of several Japanese species.*

Hypolepis

H. millefolium. New Zealand. One of the most finely divided of ferns. The long slender rhizome creeps, branching freely, sending up to 18 in. (45 cm) fronds at short intervals. Lime free conditions preferable.

Lastreopsis

L. hispida. Dryopteris-like New Zealand species, creeping rhizomes, fronds tri-quadripinnate, light golden green, rather harsh to the touch.

Matteuccia

M. germanica. Ostrich feather fern, Shuttlecock fern. Forms a very regular funnel of light green fronds up to 3 ft. (90 cm) high, fertile fronds much dwarfer within the foliar fronds. Creeps about sending dark coloured stolons in all directions, in wet soils, protecting them from erosion. The stolons form crowns at intervals, which repeat the process ad infinitum. Recently I visited a garden where I planted a dozen or so in a group, some 40 years ago. Now there is a huge stand at least 50 yards (45 m) across.

Onoclea

O. sensibilis. The sensitive fern. North America. So-called because the fronds brown at the first frost. The underground rhizomes however are absolutely hardy, anastomosing into a dense network guaranteed to protect any stream side from flood erosion. The elegant triangular to deltoid fronds, pinnate below, pinnatifid near the apex, may be up to about 18 in. (90 cm) long. The fertile fronds separate, bipinnate, the pinnae covered with sporangia, and curling round the stem to form a "bead-stick" as they are known in America, and shorter than the sterile foliar fronds.

Fig. 16. Onoclea sensibilis (the sensitive fern).

Oreopteris

O. limbosperma. Until recently named *Thelypteris limbosperma*, the mountain buckler fern. Found in woods, near mountain streams, on mountain slopes always on acid formations in the wetter counties. Strong-growing,

29

the stout creeping root-stock is very dark in colour, the uncurled fronds covered with silvery-white hairs and scales. The fronds may be from 18 in. to 4 ft. (45 cm to 120 cm) according to environment, pinnate with pinnatifid pinnae, deciduous. The blade is lanceolate, the pinnae diminish from mid-frond downwards, the lowest pinnae being deltoid, half an inch or less, a character which makes it easy to distinguish this species. Colour yellowish green, lower surface covered with yellowish glands which exude a lemon perfume—to the keen nose. The many varieties once in cultivation have all disappeared. Can only be grown in lime-free soils, but flourishes in these.

Osmunda

Two species from North America, grow up to 5 ft. (150 cm) in the wild, but seldom exceeding 3 ft. (90 cm) in Britain.

O. cinnamomea, the cinnamon fern, so called because the fertile fronds are bright cinnamon brown when ripe. The unfurled fronds are covered with silvery hairs which become reddish as the fronds unfold. The outer whorl of sterile fronds arch outwards while the longer fertile fronds stand erect in the centre. Deep, really humus-rich soil, never dry, is essential to get this fern into anything like its native stature.

O. claytonia (*O. interrupta*). So called on account of the frond, quite normal half-way up, suddenly alters its character, forming four or five shorter fertile pinnae, then reverting to the normal for the rest of the frond. At first the stems are clad with long red hairs, which eventually are shed.

O. regalis. Royal fern. A magnificent specimen for waterside planting as seen by the pool at Wisley, but in best conditions can reach 10 feet (3 m) in height. The spore-bearing fronds are intermediate, being devoted to spore production in the upper parts, purely foliar below. The green spores are viable for three or four days only at normal temperatures but can be stored a year or more in a freezer with no loss of germinating power. Needs a deep loamy soil enriched with leafmould. Among the varieties there is one with crested fronds and another with coppery-tinted young fronds.

Phegopteris

P. connectilis. Beech fern. Until recently named *Thelypteris phegopteris* but now given a genus all to itself. A lovely rhizomatous species for acid woodland, but I have seen it 2000 ft. (600 m) up in the lakeland fells, flourishing under the protection of large rocks. The fronds arise singly on long slender stems, the blade pinnate, pinnae pinnatifid. Indusium absent. The downy green surface, the two lowest pinnae sharply deflexed are identifying characters. Runs about freely in humus-rich acid soils, 9–12 in. (22.5–30 cm). Good in peat walls but can be invasive.

Phyllitis see *Asplenium scolopendrium*.

Polypodium

The common polypody. Now separated into three species on account of differences only apparent to the trained botanist. The best known is the

Fig. 17. Polypodium vulgare Cambricum.

native *P. vulgare*. Fronds rather more leathery. Linear-lanceolate, dull green, sori circular, new fronds arising in early summer. All the many varieties of polypody are splendid plants for the autumn and winter garden where their fronds remain brilliant green until early spring, when they begin to wither. There is a gap then until the new fronds arise about June. In complete shade the fronds remain green until later spring. They form surface rhizomes, and often grow in the moss on tree-trunks and on mossy rocks, or in old mortared walls.

P. v. 'Bifidum Multifidum'. Frond up to 15 in. (45 cm), pinnatisect (not quite pinnate), pinnae bifid at tips, apical branching crest to frond.

P. v. 'Cambricum'. This is the plumose form and is barren. The pinnae are deeply cut, overlapping. There are several forms.

P. v. 'Cornubiense'. So-called Cornish polypody, produces a variety of fronds, some tri- to quadripinnate, normal fronds, intermediate ones, and some incorporating all types of variation in one frond. It is as well to cut out the normal fronds whenever they appear. The fronds are longer and more dissected than *P.* 'Cambricum'.

Polystichum

The shield ferns, so called because the indusium is circular, peltate, or shield-like. The most handsome and useful of our native ferns for garden ornament, there being a remarkable range of variation, particularly in *P. setiferum.*

P. aculeatum. Hard shield fern, almost always found on basic soils. Named 'hard' on account of its leathery texture. Strong growing, up to 3 ft. (90 cm) high, more or less upright, pinnate to bipinnate, dark glossy green above, paler below. The pinnae have a typical enlarged "eared" upper basal pinnule which is found throughout the genus, giving a very characteristic appearance to the frond. The strong stock is covered with old frond bases, and when transplanting, these should be removed from the lower part of the stock, to allow young roots free access to the soil.

P. a. 'Acutilobum'. The pinnules much narrower than in the type, terminating in an acute apex. Occasionally producing bulbils. The fronds spread more or less horizontally.

P. a. 'Pulcherrimum Bevis'. After its finder Bevis. One of the most beautiful of British ferns, the graceful fronds have elongated divisions of silky texture, the pinnae curving towards the frond apex. Almost always sterile, all plants in cultivation are part of the original clone, and therefore are rather scarce.

P. setiferum. Soft shield fern. This species has given rise to more varieties than any other British fern. A very reduced list is now on record in cultivation. It has a stout rootstock, covered with old frond bases, developing subsidiary crowns by budding on frond bases. Frond wintergreen, 2–5 feet (60–150 cm) long, according to environment, bipinnate, stems covered with brown scales, glistening white in the uncurled fronds. Blade deep green, paler below, not leathery, pinnae with abundant sori. Usually found in damp woodlands, occasionally in rock clefts, usually on basic soils.

P. s. 'Congestum'. A good dwarf form, very congested, overlapping pinnae, fronds 6–9 in. (15–22 cm) high, erect. A good rock garden fern, coming true from spores.

P. s. 'Divisilobum'. The large fronds are tripinnate or evenly quadripinnate at their lower pinnae, becoming bipinnate near the frond apex. The decumbent fronds may be 3 feet (90 cm) long, up to 12 in. (30 cm) wide at the base, the whole plant covering an area 5 ft. (1.5 m) in diameter. Often bearing bulbils. There are many forms of this variety, varying in stature, and degree of dissection.

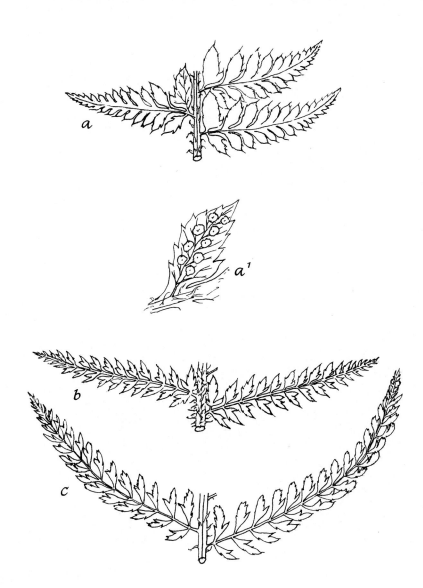

Fig. 19 *a.*   *Polystichum aculeatum* ($\times \frac{2}{3}$).

    *a*¹. *Polystichum aculeatum. Fertile pinnule, underside, enlarged, showing peltate indusia* ($\times$ 2).

    b.   *Polystichum aculeatum Acutilobum* ($\times \frac{2}{3}$).

    c.   *Polystichum aculeatum 'Pulcherrimum Bevis'* ($\times \frac{2}{3}$).

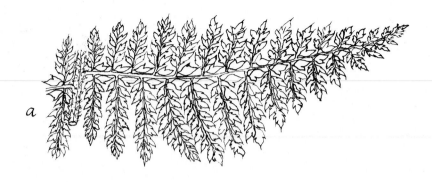

Fig. 20 *a. Polystichum setiferum divisilobum. Middle pinna. One of several forms* ($\times$ $\frac{2}{3}$).

    b. Polystichum setiferum plumoso-divisilobum. Basal pinna. Every other pinnule omitted for sake of clarity, as the pinnules overlap by half their width ($\times$ $\frac{2}{3}$).

Fig. 18. *Polystichum setiferum* '*Conspicuolobum*'.

P. s. 'Plumoso-divisilobum'. The élite of the polystichums, the fronds are quadripinnate, so finely divided and imbricate that they form plumes of mossy verdure. Two or three forms of those grown in the past are still in cultivation.

Pteris

P. cretica. Ribbon fern. A very commonly grown fern in commercial establishments. Being apogamous all the many crested varieties come true from spores, and are raised in the tens of thousands for the market. European in origin, some forms need coldhouse protection, others are hardy enough to grow in the open in Britain. Fronds 1–2 ft. (30–60 cm) long, pinnate with long terminal pinnae, sori edge the pinnae in an almost continuous line.

Thelypteris

T. hexagonoptera (*Phegopteris hexagonoptera*). Southern beech fern. North America. A delightful hardy rhizomatous species with very distinct fronds, broadly triangular to deltoid, pinnate with pinnatifid pinnae, 12–15 in. (30–45 cm) long. Slightly puberulent giving a distinct hue all its own to the fronds.

Fig. 21. Polystichum setiferum Divisilobum in mid-winter.

T. noveboracensis. New York fern. Rhizome creeping, fronds, pinnate, pubescent, narrow and tapering. An elegant species spreading rapidly in good soil. 12–24 in. (30–60 cm).

T. oreopteris, see *Oreopteris limbosperma.*

T. palustris. The marsh fern. A British native on marshes. Pinnate fronds up to 5 feet (150 cm) which arise singly or in tufts from a creeping rhizome. Grows vigorously in cultivation in suitable soils but dislikes lime. Graceful habit.

T. phegopteris see *Phegopteris connectilis.*

Trichomanes

T. speciosum. Killarney fern. One of the filmy ferns, the bi- to tripinnate fronds are so thin and translucent that the slightest drought can be fatal.

Fig. 22. Polystichum setiferum 'Divisilobum Densum'.

Can be grown to perfection in a Wardian case, or bottle garden. 3–6 in. (7.5–15 cm).

Woodwardia

Chain ferns. So-called on account of the elongated sori being arranged along the pinnae like chains of minute sausages. Strong growing woodland species requiring very moist conditions.

W. areolata. Gets its specific name on account of the areolar areas of tissue surrounded by the vein reticulum, very distinct. Barren and fertile fronds distinct. The young fronds reddish at first becoming glossy dark green later. Spreads rapidly in a congenial site.

W. radicans. This very strong growing fern has been in cultivation in Britain for over 200 years, but seldom tried in the open. It will do well enough in sheltered gardens in congenial soil, but under glass, the arching pinnate fronds may exceed 6 ft. (1.8 m) in length, the pinnae deeply pinnatifid 12 in. (30 cm) long, brilliant green. Mature fronds arch over and their tips touch the ground where they develop young plants. These can be detached and grown on. I have had a plant out-of-doors in north Lancashire for three years unharmed.

W. virginica. The stout creeping rhizome grows rapidly in swampy acid ground, being quite calcifuge. Young fronds reddish, becoming deep green, 3 ft. (90 cm) or more, ovate-lanceolate, pinnate with pinnatifid pinnae. The areoles are particularly conspicuous along the sides of the midrib. Must have really wet conditions to thrive.

The above list of species is really but a small sample of all the ferns that can be grown and are awaiting introduction from the temperate parts of the world. I have not mentioned any of which I have not had some experience at one time or another, and I fear that I shall never make the acquaintance of many that I would like to meet, but I do hope that the growing interest in ferns will increase and open the eyes of the gardening public to the wealth of beauty and grace awaiting discovery.

10. Variation in British Ferns

In the flowering plants extensive variation in flower colour and form has been achieved by hybridists over many years, special strains of food plants have revolutionised agriculture by giving greater yields, resistance to disease, and other improvements.

In the fern world variation can only take place in frond form, but many of our British species have really excelled themselves in departing from the normal in the way of cresting, increased division of the fronds, and many important details of frond structure. So much so that when the culture of ferns was at its zenith, in late Victorian times, the number of recorded variations of British ferns was well over a thousand. It became necessary to classify the many kinds of variation, and Lowe in 1890 worked out such a method. Unfortunately, owing to various factors, amongst them the incidence of two world wars, the breaking up of large estates, and dispersal of many private collections, the majority of fine old varieties have been lost, probably as many as two-thirds of them have gone for ever. Of those remaining it seemed that some modifications of Lowe's classification might be advisable, and in 1963 J. W. Dyce worked out a modified scheme for *Polystichum*, and I contributed a scheme for *Athyrium* in 1965, from which I worked out a modified system for all fern variations in 1968.

DIVISION A

Changes in frond shape. Group 1. Cristate.

This is the commonest form of variation in which the frond apex or the frond apex and pinnae, or the frond apex, pinnae and pinnules are divided to a varying degree at their tips into tassels or crests. There being so many forms of cresting, this group has been sub-divided into five sections.

(a) *Capitate.* The frond apex alone crested, pinnae not crested.

(b) *Cristate.* The frond apex crested in one plane, fan-like, the pinnae also crested. Apical crest not so wide as the frond. When the crest divisions are slender and well separated they are termed "polydactylous" (many-fingered).

(c) *Percristate*. The frond apex, the pinnae, and the pinnules are crested.

(d) *Corymbose*. The frond apex divided in several planes to give a bunched tassel, not wider than the frond itself. The pinnae are also crested. When the pinna crest are wider than the pinna they are termed "glomerate".

(e) *Grandicipital*. The terminal corymbose crest is wider than the frond itself. Pinnae crested, reduced, or absent.

Group 2. Other changes in frond shape.

(a) *Cruciate*. Each pinna reduced, often to a pair of pinnules, set at right angles forming a cross with the opposite pinna. Often combined with the cristate condition.

(b) *Ramose*. The lower part of the main frond axis divided once or more. Often combined with the cristate condition.

(c) *Congested*. Frond axis shortened so that the pinnae are very close or overlap. Also combined with the cristate condition.

(d) *Angustate*. Fronds very narrow with short pinnae which may be twisted, reflexed, or reduced to small balls.

(e) *Deltate*. Frond more or less triangular, as in an equilateral triangle.

DIVISION B

Changes in frond shape.

(a) *Plumose*. Pinnules pinnate or bipinnate, sori scanty or absent. May also be combined with the cristate condition.

(b) *Foliose*. Pinnules wider, more leafy than normal, almost confluent, often overlapping. May be combined with cristate and cruciform conditions.

(c) *Dissect*. Pinnules finely divided into teeth or bristles—setigerous. May also combine with the cristate condition.

(d) *Depauperate*. Pinnules reduced, irregular or missing. Often combined with the cristate condition.

(e) *Divisum*. A special section referring to forms of *Polystichum setiferum*, α acutilobe, β divisilobe, γ decompositae. The pinnules pinnatifid, pinnate, bipinnate, or even tripinnate. (See Dyce, *British Fern Gazette*, IX. 4.)

(f) *Heteromorphic*. All other pinnulu shapes, rounded, linear, or jagged.

It will be realised from the above analysis that the classification of fern variations can be a fairly complicated business, but when one becomes more familiar with the host of variations that can be raised from sowings, it will prove to be of real help in classifying them. In general it is true that once a fern has sported, sowings from the sport will give rise to even more elaborations. At the same time many indifferent varieties may be raised, and these should be scrapped without any hesitation. By this means there will be a gradual increase in the number of good varieties with which to adorn our gardens, and it may well be that some of those varieties which have disappeared from cultivation may appear again. If only one or two good things appear the work is well worth while.

Fig. 23. A collection of ferns in light woodland.

Appendix

The following list contains the names of some gardens where Ferns may be seen:

Borde Hill, Haywards Heath, West Sussex.

Branklyn, Perth, Tayside.

Brodick Castle, Isle of Arran, Strathclyde.

Derreen, Lauragh, Kenmare River, Co. Kerry, Eire. (Tree ferns).

Fota House, Fota Island, Cobh, Co. Cork, Eire. (Tree ferns).

Glasgow Botanic Garden, Glasgow, Strathclyde. (Large fernery under glass).

Royal Botanic Gardens, Kew, Richmond, Surrey. (Ferneries under glass).

Mount Usher, Ashford, Co. Wicklow, Eire. (Tree ferns).

Sizergh Castle, Kendal, Cumbria. (Hardy ferns).

Tatton Park, Knutsford, Cheshire. (Fernery).

Details of the British Pteridological Society may be obtained from the Secretary — J. W. Dyce, Hilltop, 46 Sedley Rise, Loughton, Essex.